D0428576

Storms and Hurricanes

Emily Bone
Illustrated by Paul Weston

Designed by Alice Reese and Sam Chandler

Additional illustrations by Kimberley Scott
Storms consultant: Dr. Roger Trend
Reading consultant: Alison Kelly, Principal Lecturer at the University of Roehampton

Contents

3 Stormy skies

4 Different weather

6 Cloudy skies

8 Wild winds

10 Cold storms

12 Ice storms

14 Electric skies

16 Whirling winds

18 Dry storms

20 The biggest storm

22 During the storm

24 After the storm

26 Tracking storms

28 Strange storms

30 Glossary

31 Websites to visit

32 Index

Stormy skies

During a storm, there are thick, dark clouds in the sky, very strong winds and often heavy rain or snow.

Sometimes, there is thunder and lightning, too.

This is a big storm in Nebraska, U.S.A.

Different weather

Storms and other kinds of weather happen all over the world. Weather is formed in the air that surrounds the Earth.

You can see weather from space. This picture shows white, swirling clouds.

The gaps between the clouds are clear skies.

The type of weather depends on how hot, cold, dry or damp the air is.

Where the air is hot and dry, the weather is sunny and there's no rain.

Cold and damp air makes cloudy, foggy, rainy or snowy weather.

Many storms happen where the air becomes hot and damp.

Other planets such as Jupiter have storms, too.

Cloudy skies

Storm clouds form when the air is warm and damp. Damp air is filled with very tiny water droplets, so small you can't see them.

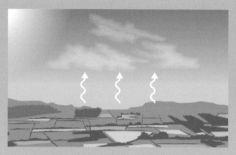

1. The Sun shines and heats up the air making the water droplets rise.

2. High above the ground, the droplets cool and join together to make clouds.

3. Inside the cloud, the droplets bump together and join to form bigger droplets.

4. Soon, the droplets of water are so big and heavy that they fall as rain.

In some parts of the world, so much rain falls at once, the ground floods.

This is Calcutta in India. It rains like this for around two months every year.

In some parts of Hawaii, U.S.A., it rains almost every day.

Wild winds

All storms come with strong winds. Wind is moving air. It happens when hot air rises and cold air rushes in to take its place.

Very strong storm winds are called gales.

These waves are crashing onto the land during a gale. Land close to the sea is often flooded.

Gales are so strong that it can be difficult for people to stand up.

Tiles are blown from roofs, and trees and electricity pylons are knocked over.

Huge waves form at sea making it very dangerous for ships and their crews.

Palm trees can bend in strong winds so they don't get blown over.

Cold storms

Snowstorms happen when the air is very cold.

Water droplets in clouds freeze into tiny ice crystals, called snowflakes.

More droplets freeze onto the flakes until they're too heavy to stay up.

Lots of snowflakes fall, covering the ground in a thick layer of snow.

This is a snowstorm in
Washington D.C., U.S.A. Snow
has filled the sky, making it
difficult to see anything.

A snowstorm with very strong
winds is called a blizzard.

Ice storms

Small balls of ice, called hailstones, form when water droplets are blown around inside a storm cloud.

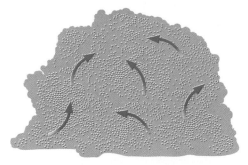

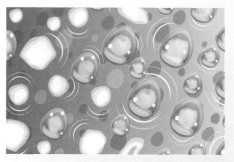

1. Droplets are blown around the cloud, where they freeze into hailstones.

2. The hailstones are blown around more. They get covered in a layer of water.

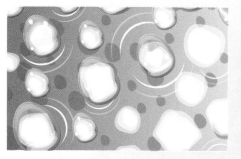

3. The water freezes into a layer around the hailstones, and they get bigger.

4. Eventually, the hailstones are so heavy, they fall to the ground.

When lots of hailstones fall from a storm cloud, it's called a hailstorm.

This giant hailstone fell in Kansas, U.S.A. It is shown here at around half its actual size.

If you cut a hailstone open, you would see the different frozen layers.

Electric skies

Thunder and lightning form inside massive storm clouds.

Damp, warm air rises high into the sky. As it cools, it turns into a storm cloud.

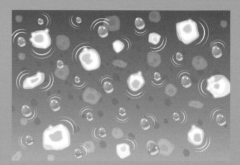

Inside the cloud, the wind swirls a mixture of hailstones and rain up and down.

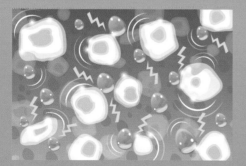

The hailstones and rain bump and rub against each other. This makes electricity.

The electricity leaps down from the cloud as a very hot flash of lightning.

Thunder is the sound
of the air quickly
heating up around
the lightning flash.

When lightning splits
like this, it is called
forked lightning.

Light travels faster than sound, so you
always see lightning before you hear thunder.

Whirling winds

Tornadoes are extremely fast, spinning winds that form inside storm clouds. In some places, they are called twisters.

A tornado's violent winds can destroy houses and farmland. This is a tornado in the U.S.A.

1. The air inside a storm cloud slowly starts to spin around and around.

2. The air spins faster and faster. The bottom of the cloud starts to grow.

3. Air is sucked up from the ground. It turns into a whirling funnel of cloud.

4. As the tornado moves along the ground it causes serious damage.

Tornadoes are called twisters because they can twist the tops from trees.

Dry storms

Dust storms happen in very hot, windy places where there is no rain, such as deserts.

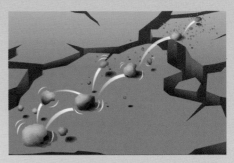

The Sun bakes the ground, making it very dry. The soil cracks into pieces.

Loose pieces of soil are blown along the ground, making them break up even more.

Soon, the loose soil becomes fine dust
and strong winds blow it into huge clouds.

Camels can close their noses
so that they don't breathe in
dust during a dust storm.

This is a dust storm in
Afghanistan. The dust has filled
the sky, blocking out the Sun.

The biggest storm

Hurricanes are huge, violent storms with very strong winds and heavy rain. They form over warm seas and can blow onto land.

The Sun heats moist air over the sea.

The moist air rises very quickly. Then it starts to spin.

As it spins, the air creates big, swirling storm clouds.

The storm gets bigger and bigger and grows into a hurricane.

This is what a hurricane looks like from space. The middle of the storm is called the eye.

In different countries, hurricanes are also known as cyclones, typhoons and willy-willies.

TYPHOON

CYCLONE

WILLY-WILLY

During the storm

Different parts of a hurricane produce different types of weather.

These palm trees in Florida, U.S.A., are being whipped by winds from a hurricane.

1. At the start of a hurricane, big swirls of dark clouds form in the sky.

2. Extremely strong winds blow, and there is heavy rain, hail, and thunder and lightning.

3. As the eye of the storm passes overhead, it is clear and sunny.

4. When the eye has moved on, clouds fill the sky. The violent weather starts again.

After the storm

When a hurricane strikes an area, it causes serious damage.

This is New Orleans, U.S.A., after Hurricane Katrina in 2005. Strong winds destroyed thousands of houses.

Hurricane winds create big waves that damage buildings on the shore.

Heavy rain makes rivers overflow their banks, flooding large areas of land.

Tracking storms

Scientists study storms to find out more about why they happen.

This weather truck has stopped under a storm cloud in Oklahoma, U.S.A.

The truck has equipment to measure wind, rain and temperature in the clouds.

Weather satellites in space look for hurricanes forming at sea.

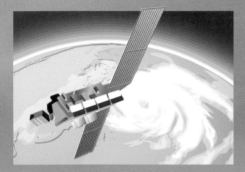

Satellites send information about the hurricane to a control room.

Computers find out where and when the hurricane might reach land.

Flags are put up in danger areas. There are warnings on the radio and television.

People leave their homes quickly so they can escape the hurricane.

Strange storms

In some parts of the world, stormy weather can do unusual things.

During an ice storm, heavy rain falls onto very cold surfaces and freezes. This photo was taken after an ice storm in Switzerland.

A tornado's strong winds can pick up fish, frogs and other small animals.

The animals are carried along, then dropped, as if they're raining from the sky.

Glossary

Here are some of the words in this book you might not know. This page tells you what they mean.

 lightning - a hot flash of electricity that jumps down from a storm cloud.

 thunder - the loud rumbling sound following a lightning flash.

 hail - small balls of ice that form inside a storm cloud.

 tornado - very fast spinning winds that look like a funnel of cloud.

 dust storm - when dry soil is blown into big clouds, blocking out the Sun.

 hurricane - a massive, violent storm with very strong winds and heavy rain.

 weather satellite - a machine in space that detects hurricanes forming.

Websites to visit

You can visit exciting websites to find out more about storms.

To visit these websites, go to the Usborne Quicklinks Website at **www.usborne-quicklinks.com** Read the internet safety guidelines, and then type the keywords **"beginners storms"**.

The websites are regularly reviewed and the links in Usborne Quicklinks are updated. However, Usborne Publishing is not responsible, and does not accept liability, for the content or availability of any website other than its own. We recommend that children are supervised while on the internet.

This is a whirling cloud of dust, called a dust devil. It's made by extremely fast, spinning winds close to the ground, like a small tornado.

Index

blizzards, 11

clouds, 3, 4, 5, 6, 10, 12, 14, 16, 17, 19, 20, 22, 23, 26

dust storms, 18-19, 30

electricity, 14

flooding, 7, 8, 25

gales, 8, 9

hail, 12-13, 14, 22, 30

hurricanes, 20-25, 27, 30

ice storms, 28

lightning, 3, 14-15, 30

rain, 3, 5, 6-7, 14, 22, 25, 26

sea, 8, 9, 20, 25, 27

snow, 3, 10-11

storm damage, 7, 8, 9, 16, 17, 24-25

Sun, 5, 6, 18, 19, 20

thunder, 3, 14, 15, 30

tornadoes, 16-17, 29, 30

warning, 27

water droplets, 6, 10, 12

weather satellites, 27, 30

wind, 3, 8, 9, 11, 12, 14, 16-17, 18, 19, 20, 22, 24, 25, 26, 29, 31

Acknowledgements

Photographic manipulation by Mike Olley
Additional design by Will Dawes

Photo credits

The publishers are grateful to the following for permission to reproduce material:
cover © Gene Rhoden/Weatherpix/Getty Images; p1© Lyle Leduc/Getty Images; p2-3 © Mike Hollingshead/Getty Images; p4 © NASA/NOAA/GSFC/Suomi NPP/VIIRS/Norman Kuring; p7 © Frederic Soltan/Sygma/Corbis; p8 © Natureslight/Alamy; p11 © ABACA USA/Press Association images; p13 © nagelestock.com/Alamy; p15 © NCAR/Science Photo Library; p16 © imagedepotpro/ Getty Images; p18-19 © Ahmad Masood/Reuters/Corbis; p21 © Fotosearch/SuperStock; p22-23 © Burton McNeely/Getty Images; p24-25 © age fotostock/SuperStock; p26 © Josh Wurman; p28-29 © Prisma Bildagentur AG/Alamy; p31 © John Warburton-Lee Photography/Alamy.
Every effort has been made to trace and acknowledge ownership of copyright. If any rights have been omitted, the publishers offer to rectify this in any subsequent editions following notification.

First published in 2012 by Usborne Publishing Ltd., Usborne House, 83-85 Saffron Hill, London EC1N 8RT, England. www.usborne.com Copyright © 2012 Usborne Publishing Ltd. The name Usborne and the devices ♀☺ are Trade Marks of Usborne Publishing Ltd. All rights reserved. No part of this publication may be reproduced, stored in a retrieval system, or transmitted in any form or by any means, electronic, mechanical, photocopying, recording or otherwise without the prior permission of the publisher. First published in America 2012. U.E.